Genre Historical Fiction

Essential Question

What was life like for people in ancient cultures?

THE TOOLMAKER

by Adrienne Jansen

illustrated by Diane Paterson

This story takes place around the year 700 C.E., when the Mayan empire was at its strongest. Mayan culture was divided into three classes: kings and nobles at the top, artisans and government workers in the middle, and farmers and unskilled workers below them. The characters in this story are from the farming class.

CHAPTER 1

The Dreamer

I lay on my stomach and smoothed the ground in front of me with my hands. Using the hard, sharp stick I kept for drawing, I carefully drew the outline of a man. I added a tall helmet so he became a warrior. Then I gave him a long spear with a sharp point, and he seemed to be brandishing it at me.

If the other boys were here, they would say, "Draw me as a warrior!" They all dreamed of being warriors. But although I drew warriors, I had a different dream. It was drawing, not fighting, that I dreamed about. I'd heard stories about the frescoes artists had painted on the walls in Tulum, close to here.

"Balam! Where are you?" My father's voice brought me back to earth. "Come on, we have lots of work to do." I stood up and scuffed out the warrior with my foot.

We had to plant all the maize before the rains came. My father was a good farmer, and he had taught me well—how to break the soil, how to plant the maize seeds, how to help them grow—but he was tough too. If I grumbled about the work, he would say, "If we don't plant maize, we will all starve. Then you'll have something to grumble about!"

It was hot, hard work swinging the hoe, cultivating the poor soil, and then planting the maize seeds. We had been working for several days, and my hands were blistered and sore.

I showed them to my father, but he barely glanced at them. "Your hands are soft," he said. "Soft hands are no good for farming." My tough father again!

I looked at the bare soil where we had planted the rows of maize. I saw all the colors of the soil, brown and ochre and red, and the way the colors ran into each other, and I wanted to paint them. But how could I, a farmer's son?

I watched my father sauntering back to the village with the other men and wished he could teach me to paint instead of plow. But he wasn't a painter.

As I approached the house where I lived with the other boys, I could hear the commotion of a ball game in progress. I heard the thump of the rubber ball as it hit the ground.

"Come on, Balam," they called out when they saw me. "Come and be a pok-a-tok champion!" Most boys loved playing pok-a-tok. They wished they could play on the long, high-walled courts that we heard were in the cities. I could play pok-a-tok as well as anyone, but I had no interest in being a champion. I wanted to be an artist. I sat and watched them for a while.

"You're a dreamer," one of them yelled.

"Lazy, more like!" laughed someone else.

They teased me again over the meal. "Eat up your tamales, Balam. They'll make you strong for dreaming!"

I took no notice. Tamales were my favorite, and I ate slowly, feeling the chilies sear my tongue, and didn't listen to the chatter.

STOP AND CHECK

How is Balam different from the other boys?

CHAPTER 2

My Treasures

My father was late calling me the next day. The other boys had already gone to work, and it was quiet in the house. I felt under my sleeping mat until my fingers found what I had hidden in a hole there—my treasures, which I only brought out when no one else was around. I knew that if the other boys saw them, they would tease me even more.

I had examined my treasures so often that I knew every tiny detail of them. The first was a small decorated cup. It was exquisite, unlike the pots and plates we used for eating. This cup, made from coiled clay and smoothed to a finish, was brightly painted with figures colored red, orange, and gray.

I ran my finger around its rim, feeling its smoothness, then put the cup to my lips and pretended to drink. I longed to make a beautiful cup like this. I wanted to learn to shape the clay and paint it in the colors of fire.

But pottery was domestic work. Women and girls made cups like this, not boys. There was no way I could ever learn to make pottery.

I tipped the cup, and my second treasure fell out. It was a chip of green rock that my father had found in the ground and given to me.

He'd held it up to the light so I could appreciate the exotic milky green of it. "What does the color remind you of?" he had asked me. I thought it looked like new corn shoots. "Or clear, deep water," he said, smiling at the stone. My tough father thought it was beautiful, too.

He told me that the rock was called jade and it came from far away in the south. People there fashioned it into beautiful jewelry and intricate carvings. Sometimes jade was buried with important people when they died.

My father told me that jade was also important for commerce because it could be traded for other goods. I wondered if my piece of jade had been lost by a trader making a long, dusty journey or sailing from faraway to conduct business in Tulum, and I made up stories about his adventures in my head. I kept my piece of jade in the cup so it didn't get lost.

I had to handle my last treasure carefully. It was a small piece of paper with writing on it. I had found it among a pile of stones beside a wall one day when my father took me to town. I knew what it was because my father had shown me a book once. It was made of folded paper and painted with small, intricate pictures.

My father had told me that to make paper, people take bark from certain trees and beat it until it is thin and soft. The book he had shown me had a cover of jaguar skin, which meant that it was very special. I had thought about that for a long time. My name, Balam, means jaguar. Maybe I was special, too.

After I had seen the book, I had wanted to make one for myself. So I had stripped some bark off a tree and beaten it thin with a stone, but it had soon fallen to pieces.

In the sunlight coming through my window, the small pictures on my treasured piece of paper were clear and bright, and there were also patterns of lines and dots. Even though I didn't know what these patterns meant, I had copied them onto the clay ground with a stick so many times that I was now a fluent writer.

I once asked my father what the patterns meant, but he didn't know. Farmers weren't taught to read.

I badly wanted to learn. I had lots of stories in my head—the stories my father told me about the time when the world was created, about the gods and animals and famous battles. I made up stories too—one about a warrior who gave up fighting and learned to carve great statues and another about a boy who made a drum from a turtle shell. I wanted to write them down so they would last forever.

One day I said to my father, "I want to learn to read and write."

But my father said, "You are a farmer's son, and you'll grow up to be a farmer. Maybe someday there will be a big upheaval and everything will change. We'll live like kings, and everyone will learn to read and write! But for now, don't think about it. Don't spend your time wanting to be a scholar. It will only make you unhappy."

STOP AND CHECK

Why does Balam hide his treasures? Why can't he make pottery or learn to read and write?

CHAPTER 3

A Surprising Journey

One day, my father roused me earlier than usual. We were going fishing. Yes! It was better than planting maize any day. Our village was near the sea, and we walked down to the beach together. I helped push the boat out, and then we both climbed in.

The huge, blue sea stretched out in front of us, and our boat seemed very small as we bobbed gently over the waves. My father helped me bait the hook on my line. "Now, keep your wits about you," he said. "We need to catch plenty of fish. And don't rock the boat!"

I held the line between my fingers. I watched the pattern of the sun on the water, the way it shifted and glinted, and the way the waves curled off the boat in white ripples. I began to make up a story in my head about a boy who caught a fish so huge that ...

Suddenly there was a sharp tug on my fingers. I jerked back so fast that the boat lurched. My father shouted, "Hey!" but he managed to shift his weight quickly so that the boat didn't capsize.

"You silly boy!" he shouted. "Stop dreaming and start fishing!"

After that, I paid attention to my line all the time. My father became quiet, and I knew he was watching me. I wondered what he was thinking.

It wasn't a good day for fishing—we didn't catch much. Finally my father said, "Let's go in. I want to go to Tulum. It's about an hour's walk from here along the coast, and we can get there and back before dark if we start now."

I knew we'd need to walk for an hour, but I was too excited about finally going there to mind. We beached the boat and set off.

At last, we saw the town, perched on the top of rocky cliffs with a wall around it on three sides. The fourth side looked out to sea. "It's a good site for defense," my father said. "You can see your enemy coming from any direction."

I thought he sounded like the village boys, always thinking about fighting. Then he laughed and said, "But you could fish every day too."

Although the town of Tulum was not very far from our village, I had never been there before, so everything was new to me as we walked through the streets thronged with people.

We came to a building that was so large I knew it must be important. I was surprised when my father went through the entrance. I didn't follow him at first—maybe we weren't allowed in—but he turned and signaled for me to come.

What I saw through the doorway made me stop in my tracks. These were the frescoes I'd heard about! The walls were covered with paintings of all kinds of figures, glowing with red and yellow. I slowly stepped inside and walked around, looking at every detail of every picture. I drew the tip of my finger over the figures and imagined what it would be like to come here every day and paint these walls.

My father came and stood beside me. "Those people are making offerings to the maize god," he said. "And that is the rain god." One by one, he talked to me about the figures on the walls.

In an alcove, I found one painting that I especially loved. It showed a man sitting holding a pot. I stared hard at it. I thought that maybe if I remembered all the details, I could draw a copy of it when I got home. But deep down, I knew that I couldn't.

The picture was too complicated, and I didn't know how to make the colors. I wished again that I had someone to teach me to make beautiful things.

STOP AND CHECK

What was the town of Tulum like, and what did Balam see there?

CHAPTER 4

Beautiful Objects

"Come, Balam!" my father called.

The morning sun glared at my laziness as I lay on my mat. I didn't want to get up. It was very hot already, though it was still early. I knew there was maize to plant, but my back was sore, and my hands were blistered.

My father called again. "Come on, Balam, it's time to get up." Then he added, "We're not planting today."

That made me get up quickly.

"Where are we going?" I asked, but he didn't respond. I didn't know what was going on. Maybe he was still angry about my carelessness in the boat the day before.

We didn't go to where the others were already working. Instead, he led the way to a clump of trees that provided shade in the stifling heat, and we sat down.

"Look at this," he said. He held out his hand to show me something lying in his palm. It was a small knife made of stone.

He passed it to me, and I held it in my hand. I could feel the surface where the stone had been carefully chipped away and the fine edge of the blade. I had seen other tools made of stone but nothing as beautiful as this.

"It's made of flint," my father said. "Flint makes very good knives because it's hard and stays sharp for a long time." Then he showed me a piece of shiny black rock with smooth faces and sharp edges. "This rock is made in the fire of volcanoes," he said. "It also makes good blades, like flint does. Today I'm going to teach you how to make tools from these rocks."

All day, my father and I worked on making a knife. He showed me how to chip the stone with another piece of flint. He showed me how to split the black rock, leaving fine, sharp edges that would make a keen blade. He showed me how to shape a knife with a small curve in the handle so that the knife wasn't just a knife anymore, it was a beautiful object too.

The sun passed across the trees, and I saw the shadows flicker on the cut edges of the stones, but I didn't think about the time.

Then my father said, "It's getting late. We have to stop now, but we'll work again tomorrow."

He put his hand on my shoulder. "Don't spend your life wanting what you cannot have, son. You and I can't be scholars or artists, but we can be good farmers. And good farmers need good tools."

I walked back to the communal house very slowly. I could hear the boys shouting and the thump of the ball, and I knew they would ask me to play. I knew they would call me lazy when I refused. They'd keep teasing me, saying, "Eat up your beans, Balam. Eat up your cassava. It'll make you strong for doing nothing!"

I didn't care. My father was right. I couldn't be a potter or a painter or a scholar. But now I knew what I could be. "I am going to be a toolmaker," I whispered to myself, "and I will work with utmost skill to make the best and most beautiful tools of all."

STOP AND CHECK

What has changed for Balam? How does this change affect how he thinks of his life?

Respond to Reading

Summarize

Use important details from *The Toolmaker* to summarize what you have learned about life in the ancient Mayan culture. Information from your graphic organizer may be helpful.

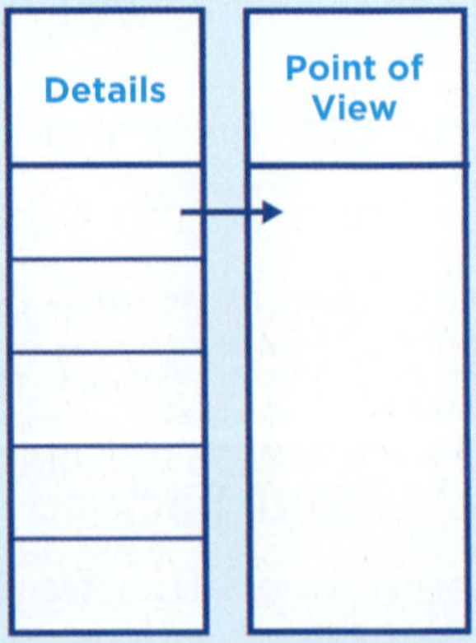

Text Evidence

1. How do you know *The Toolmaker* is historical fiction? **GENRE**

2. The author tells the story from Balam's point of view. How does this help you understand what life was like for boys in the Mayan Empire? **POINT OF VIEW**

3. What does the word *warrior* mean? What does *warrior* mean to Balam? Is it something he wants to be? The feelings he has about the word are its connotations. **CONNOTATIONS AND DENOTATIONS**

4. Write about life as it might have been for one of the other boys in Balam's village. Use details from the story to explain the other boy's point of view. **WRITE ABOUT READING**

Genre Expository Text

Compare Texts

Read on to learn more about the Mayan use of symbols and images to convey information.

MAYAN SYMBOLS

In the United States, we learn from an early age how to use the 26-letter alphabet to write words and how to use those words to create sentences.

If you lived in countries such as Russia, India, Thailand, or Israel, you would learn different alphabets. In Japan, you would learn three different alphabets.

The Mayan people were among the first people in the Americas to develop a system of writing. Their writing didn't use an alphabet like ours; they used pictures as symbols.

Mayan texts were inscribed on stone and also written in books called codices. These books were made of bark paper, cloth, and sometimes animal skins.

(t) Aaron Roeth Photography, (bkgd) Author's Image/PunchStock

As the story tells us, farmers weren't taught to read and write. Mayan scribes were an elite class. Many nobles and even kings became scribes. Their training was hard, as reading and writing the Mayan symbols was difficult work and often a word could be represented in several different ways.

DEA/G. DAGLI ORTI/De Agostini Picture Library/Getty Images

Mayan symbols were carved on stone.

Try It Yourself

Can you think of examples where we use a similar system today, conveying messages with picture symbols? In small groups, write a sentence using symbols rather than words. For example:

Challenge the other groups to decipher the meanings of your symbol writing.

Make Connections

What tells you that being a scribe was an important job within the Mayan culture? **ESSENTIAL QUESTION**

What do both the story about Balam and the article on Mayan symbols tell you about the place of writing in the ancient Mayan culture? **TEXT TO TEXT**

Focus on Genre

Historical Fiction Historical fiction uses a real setting and events in the past to tell a story. The story might use the names of characters who really existed and foreign-language words, but the details, including dialogue, are invented.

Read and Find Look for clues that reveal whether a story is set in the past, with a setting that is taken from history. You could confirm your ideas by checking an educational Internet site or reference book. Historical fiction has the usual features of fiction, such as a setting, characters, and a plot. But the events of the plot often contain historical facts that relate to a certain time period.

Your Turn

Use a graphic organizer or template to list some of the features of the setting of *The Toolmaker*. What details can you identify that the writer has used to set the scene in a realistic way? How do the descriptions help you understand what living in the Mayan culture might have been like? Choose one scene from the story and imagine you are there, for example, the fresco room at Tulum. Use an educational Internet site to discover further historical details to add to your description. Share your description with others in your group. Are your descriptions similar or very different?